Riddle-iculous Math

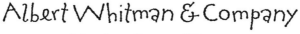

by Joan Holub

Illustrations by Regan Dunnick

Albert Whitman & Company
Morton Grove, Illinois

Library of Congress Cataloging-in-Publication Data

Holub, Joan.
Riddle-iculous math / written by Joan Holub ; illustrated by Regan Dunnick.
p. cm.
ISBN 0-8075-4996-7 (hardcover)
1. Riddles, Juvenile. 2. Mathematical recreations—Juvenile literature. I. Dunnick, Regan, ill. II. Title.
PN6371.5.H647 2003 818'.5402—dc21 2003001152

Published in 2003 by Albert Whitman & Company,
6340 Oakton Street, Morton Grove, Illinois 60053-2723.
Published simultaneously in Canada by Fitzhenry & Whiteside, Markham, Ontario.

The paintings are rendered in watercolor and pencil on paper.
The design is by Carol Gildar.

For more information about Albert Whitman & Company,
please visit our web site at www.albertwhitman.com.

A thousand thanks to Kathy Tucker for suggesting that I write riddle books.
— J.H.

To my good friend Stretch.
— R.D.

Miss Lucy had a student;
his name was Brainy Ben.
She gave him some math problems
and told him to begin.

Ben ate up the addition.
He ate subtraction, too.
He tried to eat the math book,
but it was hard to chew.

When Ben ate long division,
his giggles multiplied.
Nothing seemed to stop him
though poor Miss Lucy tried . . .

Where do math teachers eat?
On multiplication tables

How do math teachers write?
In pair-o-graphs

Munch a Bunch of Math

What is a math teacher's favorite game?
Divide and seek

What is a math teacher's favorite dessert?
A pie chart

What kind of dance can a math teacher do?
A square dance

Why do math teachers use rulers as pillows?
So they'll always know how long they've slept.

What is a math teacher's favorite season?
Sum-mer

That's Sum Creature!

What's the number of wheels
on this little bus
plus the number of arms
on an octopus
plus the number of noses
on a dozen kids
plus the number of legs
on two katydids
plus the number of spouts
on a great blue whale
plus the number of antennae
on a spotted snail
plus the number of wings
on a snow white goose
plus the number of antlers
on a grown-up moose?

4 + 8 + 12 + 12 + 1 + 2 + 2 + 2 = 43

Add these features together
to create a math teacher.
I think you'll agree
you've made some strange creature!

Spider? What Spider?

What's the number of states
in the U.S.A.
minus the number of days
in the month of May
minus the number of paws
on a grizzly bear
minus the number of legs
on the spider in your hair?

Spider!?! Eeeek!

50 − 31 = 19
19 − 4 = 15
15 − 8 = 7

Egg and Spoon Race

Take 2 steps forward,
then 1 step back.
Quick! Pass the spoon to my friend Jack.
Hop 5 steps forward,
then 2 steps right.
Hurry! Pass the spoon to my pal Dwight.
Jog 6 steps forward,
then 3 steps back.
Move! Pass the spoon to my buddy Zack.
Slide 7 steps forward,
plus 2 steps more.
Fast! Pass the spoon to the new kid, Tor.
Skip 6 steps forward, pass the spoon to Vin.
Go one step forward. Hooray! We win!

How many steps forward did the kids go
to win the egg and spoon race?

(Hint: These kids took some unnecessary steps.
Add their forward steps. Subtract their backward steps.
Don't count the 2 steps right since that wasn't a
forward or backward move.)

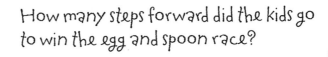

$$2 - 1 + 5 + 6 - 3 + 7 + 2 + 6 + 1 = 25$$

Win

The Pet Store

HOW much is that parakeet with green feet?

I'm feathered and friendly.
I sing and I fly.
If I'm 500 nickels,
how many quarters am I?

There are 5 nickels in a quarter.
500 ÷ 5 = 100 quarters

HOW much is that lizard in the leaf pile?

I catch bugs with my tongue.
I'm a 12-dollar reptile.
That's how many cents
if you pay penny-style?

There are 100 pennies in a dollar.
12 × 100 = 1,200 pennies

HOW much is that bunny? Hope I've got the money!

I'm soft and I'm fuzzy.
I hop fast at times.
I cost 22 dollars.
That's how many dimes?

There are 10 dimes in a dollar.
22 × 10 = 220 dimes

How many nickels
would you have to spend
to take home a new
floppy-eared bunny friend?

There are 2 nickels in a dime.
220 × 2 = 440 nickels

How much is that hamster in the window?

I'm furry and fun.
I have a short tail.
I'm 400 nickels.
Buy me—I'm for sale!
How many pennies am I?

There are 5 pennies in a nickel.
400 × 5 = 2,000 pennies

How much is that cat standing on the mat?

I'm a purr-fect pal.
I'm cute and flea-free.
If I'm 350 dimes,
how many dollars would I be?

There are 10 dimes in a dollar.
350 ÷ 10 = 35 dollars

How much is that poodle on the pillow?

I bark. I do tricks.
You can see my appeal.
I'm just 40 dollars.
Woof! Woof! What a deal!
How many quarters am I?

There are 4 quarters in a dollar.
40 × 4 = 160 quarters

How much is that tarantula in the glass tank?

I'm creepy and crawly.
I'm an interesting guy.
I cost 15 dollars.
How many pennies am I?

There are 100 pennies in a dollar.
15 × 100 = 1,500 pennies

Fortune Cookies

You will discover treasure
in an Egyptian (15 − 13)mb.
(tomb)

You will find a gr(58 − 40 − 10) surprise
hidden inside your room!
(great)

You'll build a bug with (33 − 2 − 21)tacles
with your science partner.
(tentacles)

You will read "The (59 − 54 − 2) Little Pigs"
to a kindergartner.
(Three)

You'll star in a (7 − 4 − 2)derful movie,
and it will bring you fame.
(wonderful)

You will be five minutes l(72 − 62 − 2)
for your soccer game.
(late)

You'll dream that a monster eats you
in (62 − 50 − 11) big bite. Crunch!
(one)

You will find a (11 − 8 − 1)na sandwich
packed in your school lunch.
(tuna)

Madame Crystal, FOUR-tune Teller

Your model of a
(2×2)t will win a prize
at the pioneer fair.
(fort)

Look out!
A bird is going
to poop on your
$(48 \div 12)$head!
(forehead)

You will
drop a $(100 - 96)$k
at lunch today.
(fork)

You will
$(96 - 94 + 2)$get
to take out the garbage
on purpose. This will
cause your parents to
$(7 \times 6 - 38)$get to give
you your allowance.
(forget)

You will wander into a deep,
dark $(1/2 \times 8)$est and find a
cottage full of seven dwarfs.
Oops! Scratch that unless
you are Snow White.
(forest)

You will remember to study
be$(73 - 47 - 22)$your math test
and you will get an A.
(before)

The Skip Count Cheerleaders

2, 4, 6, 8,
who do we appreciate?
8, 10, 12, ?,
our soccer coach, Ms. Morteen.

14

5, 10, 15, 20,
who do we all like, and plenty?
20, 25, 30, ?,
our lunch lady, Mrs. Dive.

35

20, 30, 40, 50,
who do we all think is nifty?
50, 60, 70, ?,
our principal, Mr. Grady.

 80

The Spud Brothers

I like things even,
it is true.
I like things that
divide by two.

Bud Spud liked things even-steven.
Judd Spud liked things odd.
So, guess which liked 4-legged chairs,
and which liked chairs tripod?
Which Spud ate 14 flapjacks,
and which ate just 11?
Which one slept 8 hours each night,
and which slept only 7?
Which Spud bounced his ball 9 times;
which bounced his 22?
Which Spud wore pants with 3 legs?
(I think that's odd, don't you?)

Bud liked the 4-legged chairs,
and Judd liked them tripod.
Bud ate 14 flapjacks,
but Judd just ate 11.
Bud slept 8 hours each night,
but Judd slept only 7.
Judd bounced the ball 9 times,
and Bud bounced it 22 times.
Judd wore pants with 3 legs.

I like things odd.
I think it's fun
that 3 – 2 leaves
a leftover one.

Look Out! Number 6 Is Hungry!

2 potato
4 potato
6 potato
8 the other potatoes!

Plenty of Pizza

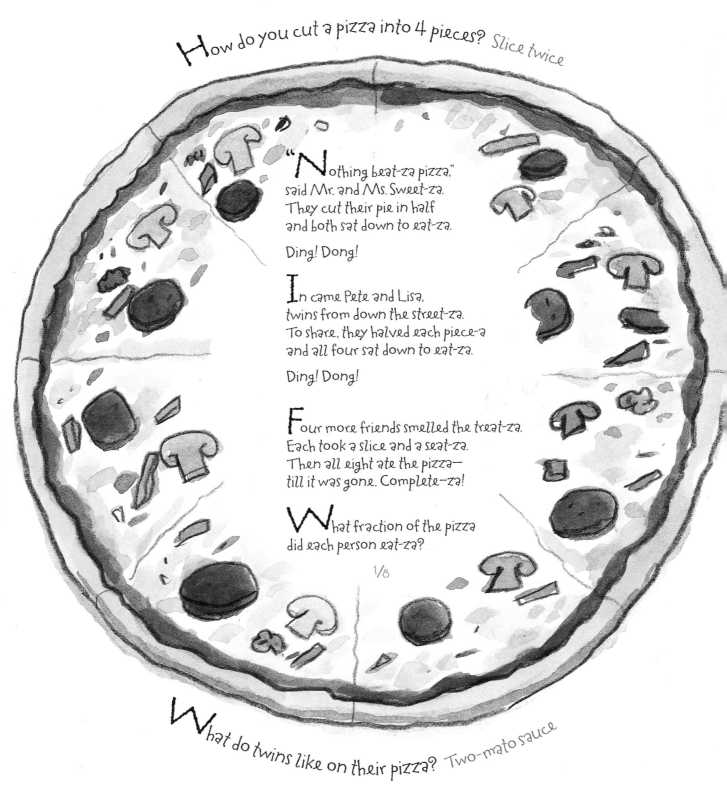

"Nothing beat-za pizza,"
said Mr. and Ms. Sweet-za.
They cut their pie in half
and both sat down to eat-za.

Ding! Dong!

In came Pete and Lisa,
twins from down the street-za.
To share, they halved each piece-a
and all four sat down to eat-za.

Ding! Dong!

Four more friends smelled the treat-za.
Each took a slice and a seat-za.
Then all eight ate the pizza—
till it was gone. Complete-za!

What fraction of the pizza
did each person eat-za?

1/8

If Mr. and Ms. Sweet-za refused to share their pizza, what fraction of the pizza would each of them eat-za?

1/2

If Mr. and Ms. Sweet-za only shared with Pete and Lisa, what fraction of the pizza would each get to eat-za?

1/4

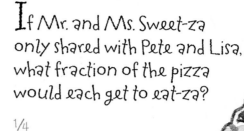

What does it take to buy a pizza? Pizza dough

What do you call a kid that likes to make pizza?

A dough-nut

Who's Faster?

Bunny rabbit hopping power
is fast at 20 miles an hour.

The fastest man can only race
at 4 miles slower than a rabbit's pace.

A horse gallops 14 miles faster than
the very fastest running man.

A cheetah's speedy quick, of course—
40 miles faster than a horse.

Do the math until you know
how fast a man, horse, and cheetah go.

Rabbit: 20 miles an hour
Man: 20 − 4 = 16 miles an hour
Horse: 14 + 16 = 30 miles an hour
Cheetah: 40 + 30 = 70 miles an hour

Which One?

A pound of bricks;
a pound of toast;
a pound of pins.
Which weighs the most?

They all weigh the same: a pound.

Up

Jack and Jill went up the hill
to fetch a gallon of water.
Their bucket only held one cup.
So how many times did they go up?

(Hint: 4 cups = 1 quart
4 quarts = 1 gallon)

$4 \times 4 = 16$

If air pressure is
measured by a barometer,
and temperature is
measured by a thermometer,
what is laughter measured by?

Perhaps a ha-ha-hometer?

Ha   Ha Ha   Ha Ha Ho

A Penny a Day

There once was a boy named Bing,
who worked for a month for the King.
One cent was the pay.
It doubled each day.
By month's end Bing was as rich as the King.

How did Bing get rich in just 30 days?
First day pay: 1 penny
Second day pay: 1 penny × 2 = 2 pennies
Third day pay: 2 pennies × 2 = 4 pennies
Fourth day pay: 4 pennies × 2 = 8 pennies
And so on...

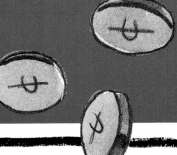

Sun	Mon	Tue	Wed	Thur	Fri	Sat
1 1¢	2 2¢	3 4¢	4 8¢	5 16¢	6 32¢	7 64¢
8 128¢	9 256¢	10 512¢	11 1,024¢	12 2,048¢	13 4,096¢	14 8,192¢
15 16,384¢	16 32,768¢	17 65,536¢	18 131,072¢	19 262,144¢	20 524,288¢	21 1,048,576¢
22 2,097,152¢	23 4,194,304¢	24 8,388,608¢	25 16,777,216¢	26 33,554,432¢	27 67,108,864¢	28 134,217,728¢
29 268,435,456¢	30 536,870,912¢	536,870,912 pennies = $5,368,709.12 (more than 5 million dollars!)				

What Do You Get if You Cross...

An 8-legged sea creature and addition?
An octo-plus

A submarine and a minus sign?
Sub-traction

Numbers and soap and water?
A math bath

Math and a bug?
An arithme-tick

A 12-inch ruler and a ball?
A foot-ball

Multiplication and a tool?
Multi-pliers

A 2 and another 2?
A tutu

A choosing game and arithmetic?
Eenie meenie miney math

A 2 and a bird?
A two-can (toucan)

A 2 and a horn?
A two-ba (tuba)

A superhero and nothing?
A super zero

Bon Voyage!

As I was going to Paris, France,
I met 11 elephants.
Each elephant had 7 plants.
Upon each plant were 7 ants.
Can you guess by any chance,
how many ants wound up in France?

$11 \times 7 \times 7 = 539?$

Nope. None.
I'm the only one who went to France.
The elephants, plants, and ants
were all going the other way.

The Metric Lunch

At lunch today young Peter Peters launched his peas quite far—9 meters.

They spattered Mary Jane O'Jeeters who then tossed grapes 11 meters.

Rice was thrown by Tyler Deeters. His toss measured 7 meters.

How many centimeters did each person's food fly?

(Hint: 1 meter = 100 centimeters)

Peter Peters:
9 × 100 = 900 centimeters

Mary Jane O'Jeeters:
11 × 100 = 1,100 centimeters

Tyler Deeters:
7 × 100 = 700 centimeters

Bunch Food Fight

Samuel Pham threw 200 grams of his chip dip (made of clams).

Pam Scrams shot 100 grams from her bowl of candied yams.

500 gooey grams of jam came from Bill Birmingham.

What fraction of 1 kilogram did each person throw?

(Hint: 1 gram = 1/1,000 kilogram)

Samuel Pham:
200 × 1/1,000 = 200/1,000 = 1/5 kilogram

Pam Scrams:
100 × 1/1,000 = 100/1,000 = 1/10 kilogram

Bill Birmingham:
500 × 1/1,000 = 500/1,000 = 1/2 kilogram

Miss Lucy's Math Library

I Love Fractions
By Henry the Eighth

We Each Have Half
By Eve N. Steven

Arithmetic Stinks!
By P. U. Math

Addition Is Fun
By Carrie Dee Five

What's 10 + 10?
By Gimme D. Sum

What's the Difference?
By Sue B. Tract

Heads or Tails
By Flip A. Coin

Learn Addition in a Minute
By Adam Fast

How to Get Quotients
By Dee Vide

Three, Six, Nine, Twelve
By Skip Count

Subtracting
By Les Stuff

I'm Always on Top of Things
By Numa Rater

One, Three, Five, Seven, Nine
By Todd Odd

Guess How Many Jellybeans Are in a Jar?
By S. T. Mate

One-fourth of JULY
By J.

Nothing and More Nothing
By Z. Row

Party Animals

When pets have a sleepover,
they celebrate with cake.
Later, they begin to snooze.
They cannot stay awake.
Cat naps start at 6 P.M.;
they all purr-purr away.
Hamsters snooze at 7 P.M.
when they're too tired to play.
Horses will not go to bed
until it's very late.
They don't fall asleep until
the A.M. time of 8.

Cats each sleep for 16 hours
on this pet party day.
Hamsters only sleep 14,
all burrowed in the hay.
Party horses just sleep 3.
But do they need more? Neigh!

When every nap is finally taken,
what time does each pet awaken?

The cats sleep until 10 A.M.
The hamsters wake up first, at 9 A.M.
The horses are the last to wake. They sleep until 11 A.M.

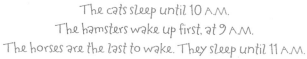

All about Us and Math

Mouths

Artichokes

Arms

M. My name is Matthew.
I'm as tall as 98 <u>m</u>arshmallows,
I weigh 33 <u>m</u>ath books,
and my family has 4 <u>m</u>ouths.

My marshmallows are ½ inch tall.
How tall am I?
98 × ½ = 49 inches

My math book weighs 2 pounds.
How much do I weigh?
33 × 2 = 66 pounds

Each person in my family
has one mouth.
How many people are in my family?
4 ÷ 1 = 4 people

A. My name is Amy.
I'm as tall as 6 South <u>A</u>mericas,
I weigh 280 <u>a</u>rtichokes,
and my family has 6 <u>a</u>rms.

On our class globe,
South America is 8 inches tall.
How tall am I?
6 × 8 = 48 inches

My artichoke weighs ¼ pound.
How much do I weigh?
280 × ¼ = 70 pounds

Each person in my family has 2 arms.
How many people are in my family?
6 ÷ 2 = 3 people

What letter does your name start with?
What objects that begin with the same letter
can you use to measure yourself and your family?

Toast

T. My name is Tucker.
I'm as tall as 10 pieces of toast,
I weigh 36 turtles,
and my family has 30 toenails.

My toast is 5 inches tall.
How tall am I?
$10 \times 5 = 50$ inches

My pet turtle weighs 2 pounds.
How much do I weigh?
$36 \times 2 = 72$ pounds

Each person in my family has 10 toenails.
How many people are in my family?
$30 \div 10 = 3$ people

H. My name is Heather.
I'm as tall as 5 toy hippos,
I weigh 46 hamsters,
and my family has 5 hairdos.

My toy hippo is 11 inches tall.
How tall am I?
$5 \times 11 = 55$ inches

The class hamster weighs
1-1/2 pounds.
How much do I weigh?
$46 \times 1 = 46$
$46 \times 1/2 = 23$
$46 + 23 = 69$ pounds

Each person in my family has one hairdo.
How many people are in my family?
$5 \div 1 = 5$ people

Toes

More Ridiculous Riddles

What's a math teacher's
favorite ice cream?

Two-tti Fruitti

What's a math teacher's
favorite hobby?

Charts and crafts

What's a game
math teachers play?

Follow the liter

Why are math
students unhappy?

Because they've got lots of problems
with no answers.

What was a 12-inch ruler
called in ancient Egypt?

A short Pharoah

What did Hercules
study in school?

Mythematics

What's the longest word in
the dictionary?

Smiles (because there's a mile
between the first and last S).

Miss Lucy had a student;
his name was Brainy Ben.
When she gave him math problems,
he ate them, one to ten.

Miss Lucy called the principal.
Miss Lucy called the nurse.
Miss Lucy called the lady
with the alligator purse.

"Math Measles," said the principal.
"Number-itis," said the nurse…

The lady with the alligator purse

Number-itis

Math Measles

Da Nurse…   The Principal

"Arithme-giggles," said the lady with the alligator purse.

What's at the end of every math book?

The letter K